TRADE MARKS 12

Includes
Logos of American
Financial Institutions

DAVID E. CARTER
EDITOR

First Printing, 1995

No design in this book may be copied
without the permission of the owner
of the mark.

Art Direction Book Co.
10 E. 39th Street
New York, NY 10016

Library of Congress Catalog Card Number:
ISBN: 0-88108-186-8
ISBN for Standing Orders: 0-910158-38-X

BOOK DESIGN: ANDI MARSHALL

OTHER BOOKS BY DAVID E. CARTER

(All these books are available from Art Direction Book Co.)
Book of American Trade Marks, Volume 1
Book of American Trade Marks, Volume 2
Book of American Trade Marks, Volume 3
Book of American Trade Marks, Volume 4
Book of American Trade Marks, Volume 5
Book of American Trade Marks, Volume 6
Book of American Trade Marks, Volume 7
Book of American Trade Marks, Volume 8
Book of American Trade Marks, Volume 9
Book of American Trade Marks, Volume 10
Book of American Trade Marks, Volume 11
Corporate Identity Manuals
Designing Corporate Identity Programs for Small Corporations
Living Logos
Evolution of Design
Logo International 1
Logo International 2
Logo International 3
Logo International 4
Logos of America's Largest Corporations
Logos of Major World Corporations
Logos of America's Fastest-Growing Companies
World Corporate Identity 1
World Corporate Identity 2
World Corporate Identity 3
How to Improve Your Corporate Identity
American Corporate Identity 1 (Sold Out)
American Corporate Identity 2
American Corporate Identity 3
American Corporate Identity 4
American Corporate Identity 5
American Corporate Identity 6
American Corporate Identity 7
American Corporate Identity 8
American Corporate Identity 9
American Corporate Identity 10
Letterheads 1
Letterheads 2
Letterheads 3
Letterheads 4
Letterheads 5
Letterheads 6
Letterheads 7
Designing Corporate Symbols
International Corporate Design Systems
How to Design Logos on Your Computer

ENTER YOUR BEST WORK
IN AMERICAN CORPORATE IDENTITY

Each Year, American Corporate Identity showcases the best new work in seven categories:

- Logos
- Letterheads
- Complete Corporate Identity Programs
- Corporate Identity Manuals
- Package Design
- Signage & Environmental Graphics
- Corporate Brochures

The book is nearly 300 pages, hard bound and mostly in full color, and is distributed worldwide .

To receive entry forms for American Corporate Identity, write to:

David E. Carter
American Corporate Identity
4100 Executive Park Drive, Suite 16
Cincinnati, OH 45241

Entry forms are sent in October of each year.

1

5

2

6

PARALAX™
NEW PERSPECTIVES IN WORKSPACE

3

Innervision

7

THE
DENVER
EXECUTIVES
CLUB

4

8

10

11

12

13

17

14

18

15

19

16

20

DRUMS ALONG THE ROCKIES

21

22

23

24

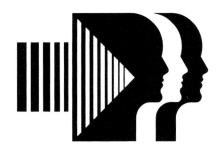

37

38

39

40

41

42

43

44

45

46

47

48

49

53

Gina Sophia DeCagna

50

54

I S F
SYSTEMS
CORPORATION

51

HELIPORT
SYSTEMS
INC.

55

52

56

57

58

59

60

61

65

62

66

63

67

64

MONOCID

68

69

73

77

74

78

75

79

76

80

18

81

82

83

84

85

89

86

90

87

91

88

92

93

94

95

96

97

98

99

100

22

101

102

103

104

INDUSTRIA

105

106

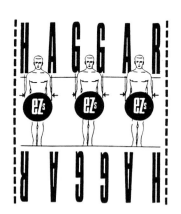

107

108

117

118

119

120

121

125

22

126

123

127

124

128

129

SHOWCASE
KITCHENS

130

131

132

133

137

134

138

135

139

136

140

DOUGLAS SYMES
BARRISTERS
& BRISSENDEN
SOLICITORS

141

Workspirit

142

143

MODATECH

144

145

149

146

150

147

151

148

152

153

AMTEST

154

155

First

156

FirstImage

157

158

159

160

161

162

163

164

165

166

167

The Adaskin Society

168

177

178

179

180

181

185

182

186

183

187

184

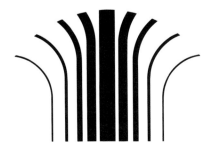

188

201

202

203

204

205

209

206

210

207

Malloy Industries Inc.

211

208

NISHMAT·נשמת

212

213

214

215

216

CYGNUS

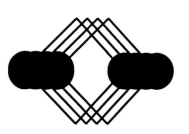

226

227

228

229

230

234

231

235

232

PEREGRINE
SOLUTIONS

236

237

238

239

240

241

245

242

246

243

247

244

248

46

250

251

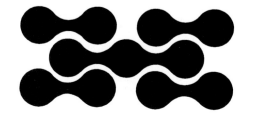

252

241 State of Iowa
   Design: Sayles Graphic Design

242 State of Iowa
   Design: Sayles Graphic Design

243 State of Iowa
   Design: Sayles Graphic Design

244 State of Iowa
   Design: Sayles Graphic Design

245 State of Iowa
   Design: Sayles Graphic Design

246 State of Iowa
   Design: Sayles Graphic Design

247 State of Iowa
   Design: Sayles Graphic Design

248 State of Iowa
   Design: Sayles Graphic Design

249 State of Iowa
   Design: Sayles Graphic Design

250 TexasFirst
   Design: Logo Bank

251 Fitzpatrick Nurseries
   Design: Logo Bank

252 Future Concepts
   Design: Logo Bank

253

257

254

258

255

259

256

260

261

262

263

264

265

ACHCA
American College of Health Care Administrators

269

266

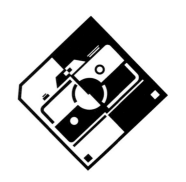

270

267

Automated Assemblies Corporation

271

268

272

273

Scott Hill

274

275

Ptech Inc.

276

Advanced Technology Group

286

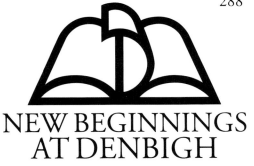

287

288

301

CITICORP CENTER
Concierge

302

303

304

PANTHEON
ARCHITECTURAL MILLWORK

305

Austin's
FINE JEWELRY

306

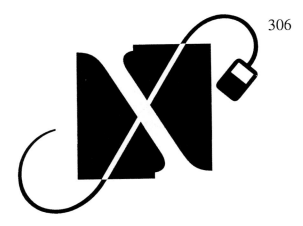

307

308

309

310

311

KramerBrothers

312

Seattle
Goodwill

313

317

314

KEVIN BAKER

**LANDSCAPES &
STONESCAPES**

318

Twin Palms

315

ROCKY MOUNTAIN
CONCRETE PRODUCTS, INC.

319

316

HIGH
TECH

CONSTRUCTION

320

321

322

323

324

325

LOS ANGELES DESIGN COMPANY

326

tender loving care for your teeth

Anita Paulus, DDS

327

328

IOWA RIVER CITIES

329

TPTA

T E N N E S S E E
Physical Therapy Association

330

Curlee

Outdoor Lighting Products

331

Community
Health
Care
Clinic

332

JOCKEY

TECH

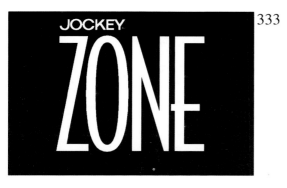

333

G I B S O N · G R O U P
advertising resource and design

334

335

336

337

home innovations

338

339

B I G
H A N D

340

341

AS / 400
ROSS

342

343

COROMANDEL

YOUR ISLAND IN THE STREAM

344

PackNet™

PMMI'S ON-LINE WORLD OF PACKAGING TECHNOLOGY

345

346

347

348

361

365

362

366

363

367

364

368

369

370

371

372

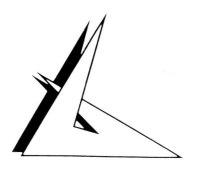

381

382

383

384

385

389

386

390

387

391

388

392

393

394

395

SHAPE UP

396

397

401

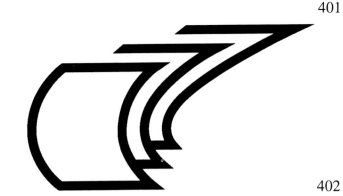

398

402

399

403

400

404

405

406

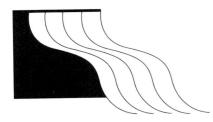

407

A Shade Beyond

408

CHESTERWOOD
ESTATE & MUSEUM

409

The Jon Lewis ORCHESTRA

413

SEA 'SCAPE
YACHT CHARTERS

410

CRYSTAL
WATER CO.

414

411

LAKE COUNTY

Guiding Your Health

GENERAL HEALTH DISTRICT

415

San patricio PLAZA

412

RDI Software Technologies, Inc.

416

Precision
AUDIO & HOME ENTERTAINMENT

417

418

419

420

The
Bridge
Fund
for
Growth

MAFMA
MIDWEST ADVANCED FOOD
MANUFACTURING ALLIANCE

PRIVATE BANKING

NORTHWAY
MALL

Contracting
Services

DOLPHIN
F O R M S ™
The Intelligent System

429

LAKE ANNE PLAZA

430

431

432

InPhyNet

MEDICAL MANAGEMENT SM

BROOKS

TELECOMMUNICATIONS
INTERNATIONAL

ACCOLADES™

441

442

443

444

445

449

446

450

447

451

448

452

453

454

455

456

BroadVision

of France

467

high five entertainment

468

THE ACAPPELLA COMPANY®

469

CAMBRIDGE
FRIENDS
SCHOOL

458 Sparc Master's Sparc Resurgent
Design: Chikamura Design

459 Joan Ussery
Design: Design One

460 The Foundation Center
Design: David Schiffer Design, Inc.

461 Distinctive Paint Design
Design: Freestyle Studio

462 BroadVision
Design: Chikamura Design

463 Cresc - Homefires
Design: Disegno

464 Cresc
Design: Disegno

465 Council of State Governments
Design: Disegno

466 Ariel of France
Design: Disegno

467 High Five Entertainment
Design: Jackson Design

468 The Acappella Company
Design: Jackson Design

469 Cambridge Friends School
Design: Marc English Design

Touch
The Heart of
the U.S.

VISIT
MID·AMERICA

COLLEGE OF
BUSINESS
OHIO UNIVERSITY

At the Lincoln Theater

Ohio River Bank

Mount Vernon
Christian School

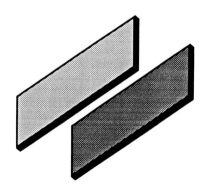

Thai-
Finnish

CHAMBER OF COMMERCE

478

479

480

481

470 US Department of Commerce
Design: Tobias Oleson Design

471 SKAGIT-Mount Vernon Kiwanis Club
Design: Prime West, Inc.

472 Mount Vernon Christian School
Design: Prime West, Inc.

473 M^2 - McCown Marshall, Inc.
Design: M^2

474 Ohio University
Design: M^2

475 Ohio River Bank
Design: M^2

476 Oil Center
Design: M^2

477 Thai-Finnish Chamber of Commerce
Design: M^2

478 Canstar Sports USA
Design: Visual Marketing Associates, Inc.

479 Univera
Design: Graphic Concepts Group

480 Accusight
Design: Julia Tam Design

481 Consilidated Freightways, Inc.
Design: Kenneth M. Wood Jr.

482

Intelligent Terminals

486

MADERA del PRESIDIO

483

487

484

488

485

SJ PACKAGING

489

490

491

492

493

494

498

495

Gifts and Goodies Unlimited

499

BIG FUTURE

496

500

497

501

502

503

504

505

Logos of American Financial Institutions

Over the years, I have received many requests to produce a book showing logos of financial institutions. This section of the book is especially devoted to logos of American banks, savings & loans and similar financial institutions.

CommerceAmerica Banking Company
Jeffersonville, IN

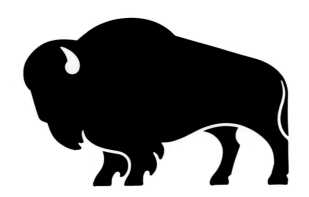

CommerceAmerica

Bright Banc Savings Association
Dallas, TX

First Union National Bank of Georgia
Columbus, GA

First American Bank
Boston, MA

United New Mexico
Albuquerque, NM

First Service Bank
Leominster, MA

American National Bank & Trust Company
Chattanooga, TN

First Bank Minneapolis
Minneapolis, MN

International Bank of Commerce
Laredo, TX

INTERNATIONAL BANK OF COMMERCE

Old Phoenix National Bank
Medina, OH

OLD PHOENIX NATIONAL BANK

First Citizens Bank
Columbia, SC

First Citizens Bank

Taunton Savings Bank
Taunton, MA

Barnett Bank
St. Augustine, FL

Citizens Bank & Trust Company
Paducah, KY

Sun First National Bank of Polk County
Winter Haven, FL

Sun First National Bank of Polk County

Naper Bank
Naperville, IL

Naper Bank

The Peoples Bank
Bloomington, IL

THE PEOPLES BANK

Fifth Third Bank
Cincinnati, OH

Dollar Dry Dock Savings Bank
White Plains, NY

Central Bancorporation, Inc.
Denver, CO

First National Bank
Elkhart, IN

Evergreen Federal Savings Bank
Charleston, WV

Interwest Bank of Arizona
Tucson, AZ

Inter**West**

Bank of Arizona

Civic Savings
Portsmouth, OH

Mid-America Federal
Columbus, OH

Mid★America Federal

Peoples Bank of Olive Hill
Olive Hill, KY

First Kentucky
Central City, KY

MidAmerican Bank & Trust Company
Shawnee Mission, KS

Cape Cod Bank & Trust Company
Hyannis, MA

Bank of Newport
Newport, RI

National Bank of Alaska
Anchorage, AK

Beverly Savings Bank
Beverly, MA

The Mid-City National Bank of Chicago
Chicago, IL

Central Bank & Trust Company
Lexington, KY

Federal Home Loan Bank of San Francisco
San Francisco, CA

**Federal Home
Loan Bank of
San Francisco**

Farmers & Merchants Bank of Central California
Lodl, CA

Central Bank
Monroe, LA

CentraBank

Merchants Bancorp, Inc.
Aurora, IL

National Bancshares Corporation of Texas
San Antonio, TX

Home & City Savings Bank
Albany, NY

First National Bank
Clayton, MS

First National Bank
of St. Louis County

Society Bank of Eastern Ohio
Canton, OH

Jefferson National Bank
Charlottesville, VA

National Bank of Commerce
Birmingham, AL

**National Bank
of Commerce**

American State Bank
Kenosha, WI

Marine Bank
Erie, PA

US Bank
Seattle, WA

US BANK

The Drovers & Mechanics Bank
York, PA

The Savers Bank
Littleton, NH

Putnam Trust Company
The Bank of Greenwich
Greenwich, CT

Columbus Bank & Trust
Columbus, GA

The Roslyn Savings Bank
Roslyn, NY

Central National Bank
Canajoharie, NY

Jefferson Bank
Peoria, IL

Durfee Attleboro Bank
Fall River, MA

Manufacturers Hanover
New York, NY

Megabank
Miami, FL

First National Bank
San Diego, CA

Hamilton Bank
Lancaster, PA

Lawrence Savings Bank
Lawrence, MA

First National Bank of Elgin
Elgin, IL

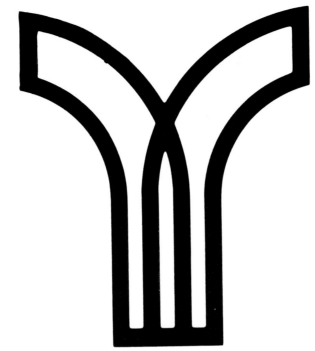

Meridan Bancorp, Inc.
Reading, PA

Lake Shore National Bank
Chicago, IL

NBD Highland Park Bank
Highland Park, IL

The Merchants Bank of New York
Broadway, NY

New Jersey Savings Bank
Somerville, NJ

NEW JERSEY
SAVINGS BANK

The Mitsubishi Bank of California
Los Angeles, CA

Cardinal Federal
Owensboro, KY

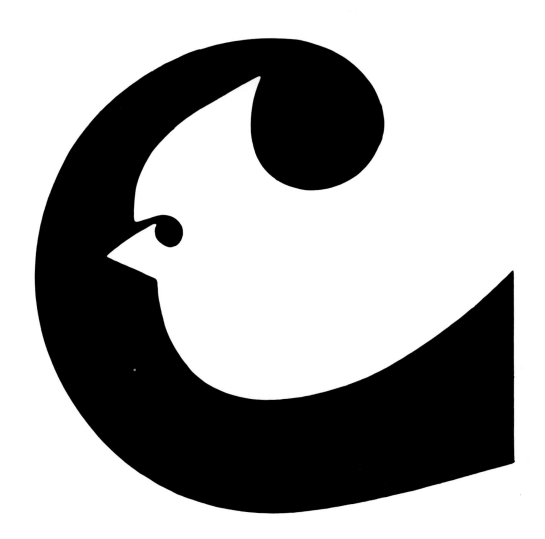

First Banks
Minneapolis, MN

First Bank System

First Interstate Bank of Texas
Houston, TX

First Interstate Bank

First National in Palm Beach
Palm Beach, FL

First National in Palm Beach
a Division of Southeast Bank, N.A.

First Wisconsin National Bank of Eau Claire
Eau Claire, WI

FIRST WISCONSIN
EAU CLAIRE

110

Bank of Pennsylvania
Reading, PA

BANK OF PENNSYLVANIA®

First National Bank at Lubbock
Lubbock, TX

First National Bank

Mid American National Bank & Trust Company
Bowling Green, OH

Bank of Pensacola
Pensacola, FL

Farmers & Merchants State Bank
Wauseon, OH

Citibank Arizona, a Subsidary of Citicorp
Phoenix, AZ

Chemung Canal Trust Company
Elmira, NY

LaJolla Bank & Trust Company
San Diego, CA

Puget Sound Bank
Tacoma, WA

Home Bank
Signal Hill, CA

Magna Group, Inc.
Belleville, IL

National Bank of Commerce Company
Charleston, WV

National Banc of Commerce Company

Middletown Savings Bank
Middletown, CT

Middletown Savings Bank

New Brunswick Savings Bank
New Brunswick, NJ

NEW BRUNSWICK SAVINGS BANK

First Security National Bank & Trust Company
Lexington, KY

FIRST SECURITY
NATIONAL BANK & TRUST COMPANY

First National Bank of South Miami
South Miami, FL

Connecticut Savings Bank
New Haven, CT

Bank South Corporation
Atlanta, GA

Manufacturers Bank
Detroit, MI

Texas American Bank, Fort Worth NA
Fort Worth, TX

The Citizens & Southern Corporation
Atlanta, GA

The Liberty Bank
Middletown, CT

Key Bank of Southeastern New York
Newburgh, NY

First Wisconsin, Milwaukee
Milwaukee, WI

Crestar Bank
Norfolk, VA

The Republic National Bank of New York
New York, NY

REPUBLIC NATIONAL BANK OF NEW YORK

A SAFRA BANK

Provident Bank of Maryland
Baltimore, MD

Ohio Bancorp
Youngstown, OH

First Illinois Corporation
Evanston, IL

Peoples Bank of Lakeland
Lakeland, FL

 **Peoples Bank of Lakeland**

First Wachovia Corporation
Winston-Salem, NC

FIRST WACHOVIA

The First National Bank of Anchorage
Anchorage, AK

First National Bank
of Anchorage

NCNB National Bank
Charlotte, NC

Farmers and Mechanics National Bank
Frederick, MD

Commerce Bancshares, Inc.
Kansas City, MO

The Bryn Mawr Trust Company
Bryn Mawr, PA

Liberty Bank
Honolulu, HI

Plaza Bank of Commerce
San Jose, CA

PLAZA BANK
OF COMMERCE

Signet Bank
Richmond, VA

The National Bank of Washington
Washington, DC

Charter Bank
Sparta, IL

First National Bank of Springfield
Springfield, IL

Commercial Charter Bank
Santa Ana, CA

First United National Bank & Trust
Oakland, MD

Cheshire County Savings Bank
Keene, NH

Bank of A. Levy
Ventura, CA

The First National Bank of Pikeville
Pikeville, KY

Glastonbury Bank & Trust
Glastonbury, CT

Glastonbury Bank & Trust

First City National Bank of Arlington
Arlington, TX

First City
National Bank
of Arlington

Vermont National Bank
Brattleboro, VT

Burke & Herbert Bank & Trust Company
Alexandria, VA

Southwest Bank
St. Louis

The Principal Mutual Life Insurance Company
Des Moines, IA

Irwin Union Bank & Trust Company
Columbus, IN

Farmers Bank & Capital Trust Company
Frankfort, KY

Farmers Bank
& Capital Trust
Company

Home Owners Federal Savings
Burlington, MA

Rockland Trust Company
Rockland, MA

Valley Bank
Idaho Falls, ID

The Chatham Trust Company
Morristown, NJ

Pioneer Bank, a LANE Bank
Chicago, IL

The First National Bank of Atlanta
Atlanta, GA

FIRSTATLANTA

Guaranty-First Trust Company
Waltham, MA

The Bank of Baltimore
Baltimore, MD

Kentucky National Bank of Kenton County
Covington, KY

General Bank
Los Angeles, CA

Mercantile Bancorporation, Inc.
St. Louis, MO

AmSouth Bank
Birmingham, AL

AmSouth®

Liberty National Bank
Louisville, KY

**Liberty
National
Bancorp,
Inc.**

The Security National Bank
Shreveport, LA

**Security
National
Bank**

Malden Trust Company
Malden, MA

Malden Trust
c o m p a n y

SallieMae
Washington, DC

SallieMae

Dominion Bankshares Corporation
Roanoke, VA

DOMINION
BANK

Knutson Mortgage Corp.
Burlington, MA

KNUTSON
MORTGAGE CORPORATION
A Home Owners Company

Sun Savings and Loan Association
Burlington, MA

SUN SAVINGS & LOAN ASSOCIATION, F. A.
A Home Owners Company

Charter Oak Federal Savings Bank
Columbus, OH

Charter Oak^{SM}
FEDERAL SAVINGS BANK
Established 1880

BankEast
Manchester, NH

BankEast
The right direction for you.

Palmetto Federal of South Carolina
Beaufort, SC

PALMETTO
FEDERAL

Firstier
Omaha, NE

Century Federal Savings
Pasedena, CA

🌹 Century Federal Savings

Sun Bank of Tampa Bay
Tampa, FL

First National Bank & Trust Company
Stuart, FL

Bank of America
San Francisco, CA

Pinnacle West Capital Corporation
Pheonix AZ

PINNACLE WEST
CAPITAL CORPORATION

Shawmut
Boston, MA

Caribank
Fort Lauderdale, FL

First Hawaiian Bank
Honolulu, HI

Michigan National Bank
Farmington Hills, MI

Chase Manhattan Bank
New York, NY

Premier Bancorp
Baton Rouge, LA

First National Bank of El Dorado
El Dorado, AR

First National Bank of El Dorado

American Bank
Shreveport, LA

United Missouri Bancshares, Inc.
Kansas City, MO

Suntrust Banks, Inc.
Atlanta, GA

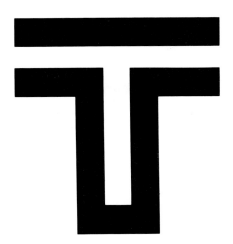

Virginia Federal Savings and Loan
Richmond, VA

Workingmens Cooperative Bank
Boston, MA

Sea Island Bank
Statesboro, GA

Frost National Bank
San Antonio, TX

Cullen/Frost Bankers, Inc.®

Florida Federal
St. Petersburg, FL

Pontchartrain Bank
Metairie, LA

Lincoln National Bank
Fort Wayne, IN

Sunrise Federal
Newport, KY

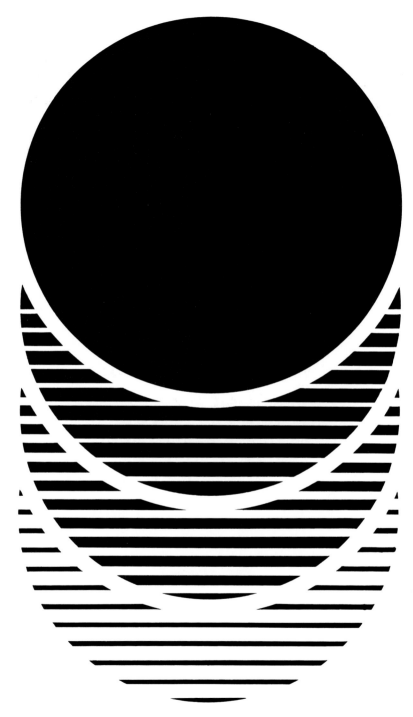

One Bank
Little Rock, AR

ONEBANK

The American Banks
Jacksonville, FL

The American Banks

Northwest Bank
Oklahoma City, OK

T. Rowe Price Associates, Inc.
Baltimore, MD

Marshall & Ilsley Bank
Milwaukee, WI

Maryland National Bank
Baltimore, MD

MARYLAND NATIONAL BANK

The Cumberland
A Federal Savings & Loan Association
Louisville, KY

First National Bank of Central Jersey
Bridgewater, NJ

FIRST NATIONAL BANK
OF CENTRAL JERSEY

Pioneer Bank and Trust Company
Shreveport, LA

Pioneer Bank
& TRUST CO.

Fed One Savings BAnk
Wheeling, WV

Rainier Bancorporation
Seattle, WA

American Savings
Salt Lake City, UT

Rhode Island Hospital Trust National Bank
Providence, RI

Horizon Bank
Morristown, NJ

PNC Financial Corp.
Pittsburg, PA

Pittsburg National Bank
Pittsburg, PA

Fortune Savings Bank
Clearwater, FL

First Florida Bank, N.A.
Tampa, FL

FIRST FLORIDA
BANK

Park National Bank
Minneapolis, MN

OF ST. LOUIS PARK

Comerica, Inc.
Detroit, MI

Commonwealth National Bank
Harrisburg, PA

Provident National Bank
Philadelphia, PA

Trustmark National Bank
Jackson, MS

Great Western Financial Corporation
Beverly Hills, CA

GREAT
WESTERN

GW

Great Western Financial Corporation

National Bank of Detroit
Detroit, MI

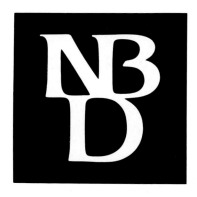

First Virginia Banks Inc.
Falls Church, VA

Bank of New Hampshire National Association
Manchester, NH

Third National Bank
Knoxville, TN

First American Bank & Trust of Louisiana
Monroe, LA

First National Bank of Omaha
Omaha, Nebraska

First Guaranty Bank and Trust Company
Jacksonville, FL

Orange Bank
Orlando, FL

Dow Jones & Company, Inc.
New York, NY

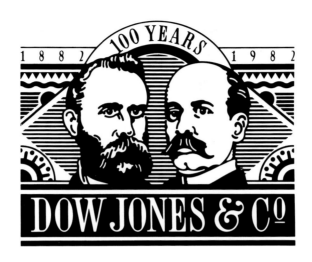

First Fidelity Bancorporation
Newark, NJ

First Federal Savings of Austin
Austin, TX

Midland Financial Savings and Loan
Des Moines, IA

AmBank American Bank
Baton Rouge, LA

Home Federal Savings & Loan Assoc.
San Diego, CA

HOME FEDERAL

Southeast Banking Corp.
Miami, FL

First National Bank of Maryland
Baltimore, MD

First Security National Bank & Trust Co.
Lexington, KY

Eliot Bank
Boston, MA

M-Corp Momentum Company
Dallas, TX

First National Bank of Grayson
Grayson, KY

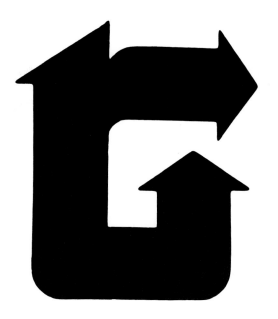

Home Federal Savings & Loan
Ashland, KY

M&T Bank
Buffalo, NY

The Arizona Bank
Phoenix, AZ

Norwest Corporation
Minneapolis, MN

CoreStates Financial Corp.
Philadelphia, PA

Piedmont Trust Bank
Martinsville, VA

Valley Bank
Madison, WI

Ameribank
Savannah, GA

Citibank
New York, NY

Marine Midland Bank
New York, NY

The Huntington National Bank
Columbus, OH

Midlantic National Bank
Edison, NJ

MIDLANTIC

Interstate Bank of Commerce
Miami, FL

 INTERSTATE BANK OF COMMERCE

Raleigh Federal Savings Bank
Raleigh, NC

 Raleigh Federal
SAVINGS BANK

First Pennsylvania Bank
Philadelphia, PA

 FIRST PENNSYLVANIA CORPORATION

Plano Bank & Trust
Plano, TX

Thunderbird Bank
Phoenix, AZ

Valleybank & Trust Company
Chambersburg, PA

The Ramapo Bank
Wayne, NJ

Crossland Savings
Brooklyn, NY

First National Bank
Dayton, OH

MeraBank
Phoenix, AZ

Continental Bank
Salt Lake City, UT

Texas State Bank
McAllen, TX

Texas State Bank

Sovran Bank
Norfolk, VA

Crestar Financial Corporation
Richmond, VA

Albany Savings Bank
Albany, NY

Bank One, Lexington
Lexington, KY

American Security Bank
Washington, DC

AMERICAN
SECURITY
BANK ®

Eastover Bank for Savings
Jackson, MS

Eastover
Eastover Bank For Savings

The State First National Bank
Texarkana, AR

State First National Bank
OF TEXARKANA

One Valley Bank
Charleston, WV

ONE VALLEY
BANK

New World Bank
Boston, MA

Lake City Bank
Warsaw, IN

Baltimore Federal Financial
Baltimore, MD

Sunwest Bank of Albuquerque
Albuquerque, NM

SUNWEST BANK

First National Bank
Orangeburg, SC

Citizens State Bank
Owensboro, KY

Citizens State Bank

The Texarkana National Bank
Texarkana, TX

Midland Bank
Paramus, NJ

Landmark Savings Bank
Indianapolis, IN

NCNB National Bank
Tampa, FL

Liberty Savings Bank
Macon, GA

The Merchants National Bank
& Trust Company of Syracuse
Syracuse, NY

Trustcorp Bank, Ohio
Toledo, OH

Source Bank
South Bend, IN

Merchants National Corporation
Indianapolis, IN

MERCHANTS NATIONAL BANK & TRUST COMPANY

Morris Savings Bank
Morristown, NJ

First RepublicBank
Dallas, TX

Benton Inter-City Bank
Benton Harbor, MI

The Children's Bank
New York, NY

First Bank & Trust Compnay
Creve Coeur, MO

The First Women's Bank
New York, NY

Kansas State Bank & Trust
Wichita, KS

Kansas State Bank & Trust

California Overseas Bank
Beverly Hills, CA

California Overseas Bank

Harvest Savings Bank
Dubuque, IA

First Interstate Bancorp
Los Angeles, CA

First National Bank & Trust Company
Carbondale, IL

Bankers Trust Company
New York, NY

Bankers Trust Company

Union Federal Savings Bank
Indianapolis, IN

Hardwick Bank and Trust Company
Dalton, GA

Wilmington Savings Fund Society
Wilmington, DE

The Calcasieu Marine National Bank
Lake Charles, LA

First National Bank of Louisville
Louisville, KY

Merchants National Bank
Vicksburg, MS

Apple Bank for Savings
New York, NY

The Benj. Franklin Federal Savings
& Loan Association
Portland, OR

National Bank of Boyertown
Boyertown, PA

Peoples Heritage Federal Savings
Salina, KA

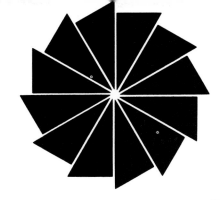

United Jersey Bank Commercial Trust
Jersey City, NJ

First Chicago Corp., The First National Bank of Chicago
Chicago, IL

Mellon Bank
Pittsburgh, PA

SunTrust Banks, Inc.
Atlanta, GA

United Jersey Banks
Princeton, NJ

United Jersey Banks
Members FDIC

SouthTrust Corporation
Birmingham, AL

Cumberland Valley National Bank & Trust Company
London, KY

Cumberland Valley National Bank

Vistar Bank
Lincoln, NE

U.S. Bancorp
Portland, OR

Penn Bancorp
Oil City, PA

Binghamton Savings Bank
Binghamton, NY

Binghamton Savings Bank

Peoples Bank
Marietta, OH

Affiliated Banc Group, Inc.
Morton Grove, IL

The Boston Five
Boston, MA

Citytrust
Bridgeport, CT

Fort Wayne National Bank
Fort Wayne, IN

**FORT WAYNE
NATIONAL BANK**

Goldome
Buffalo, NY

First Seneca Bank
Oil City, PA

Bank of the Orient
San Francisco, CA

City National Bank of Fort Smith
Fort Smith, AR

The Connecticut Bank
& Trust Company
Hartford, CT

BankAtlantic
Fort Lauderdale, FL

Old National Bank in Evansville
Evansville, IN

Peoples Bank & Trust Company
Indianapolis, IN

peoples bank

American Savings Bank
White Plains, NY

First Citizens Bank
Raleigh, NC

FIRST CITIZENS BANK

Cortland Savings & Banking Company
Cortland, OH

Rapides Bank & Trust Company
Alexandria, LA

Blue Ridge Bank & Trust Company
Kansas City, MO

Lorain National Bank
Lorain, OH

Progressive Consumers Federal Credit Union
Saugus, MA

Florida National Bank
Jacksonville, FL

City Bank & Trust Company
Jackson, MI

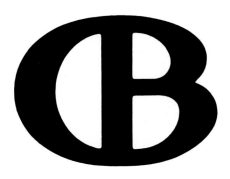

Lafayette Bank & Trust Company
Lafayette, ID

First Victoria National Bank
Victoria, TX

Gateway Bank
South Norwalk, CT

First National Bank of Toledo
Toledo, OH

Merchants Bank
Allentown, PA

Merchants
Bank

First National Bank & Trust Company
Columbus, NE

Petersborough Savings Bank
Petersborough, NH

Mid-Hudson Savings Bank
Fishkill, NY

USBI Marketing
Manchester, NH

Sunburst Bank Corporate Administration
Grenada, MS

The First National Bank
Shreveport, LA

Citizens National Bank
Meridian, MS

First National Bank of Southwestern Ohio
Middletown, OH

Hudson United Bank
Union City, NJ

Jefferson Bank
Philadelphia, PA

Lockport Savings Bank
Lockport, NY

United National Bank & Trust Company
Canton, OH

Calumet National Bank
Hammond, IN

State Glenview Bank
Glenview, IL

The Troy Savings Bank
Troy, NY

First American Bank of Virginia
McLean, VA

1st AMERICAN BANK

North Fork Bank
Mattituck, NY

Beckley National Bank
Beckley, WV

Farmers & Merchants National Bank
Winchester, VA

Waukesha State Bank
Waukesha, WI

Liberty State Bank & Trust
Troy, MI

Vermont Federal Bank
Burlington, VT

Bank of Hawaii
Honolulu, HI

Avco Financial Services
Irvine, CA

First National Bank of Mount Prospect
Mount Prospect, IL

First National Bank
of Mount Prospect

First National Bank in Bartlesville
Bartlesville, OK

**First National Bank
in Bartlesville**

American National Bank
St. Joseph, MO

United National Bank
Plainfield, NJ

Maine National Bank
Portland, ME

Morgan Guaranty Trust Company
New York, NY

JPMorgan

Southstate Bank
Brockton, MA

Colonial BancGroup
Montgomery, AL

Berkshire County Savings Bank
Pittsfield, MA

Indiana National Corporation
Indianapolis, IN

Bristol Savings Bank
Bristol, CT

First of America Bank Corporation
Kalamazoo, MI

The Dollar Savings & Trust Company
Youngstown, OH

Valley Bancorporation
Appleton, WI

Great Country Bank
Ansonia, CT

Security Bank
Salisbury, NC

Security Bank

First City Bank of Richardson
Richardson, TX

First City
Bancorporation
of Texas, Inc.

Consolidated Bank
Hialeah, FL

Salem Five
Salem, MA

Independence Bank
Encino, CA

First National Bank
San Antonio, TX

The Idaho First National Bank
Boise, ID

Union Bank & Trust Company
Montgomery, AL

UNION BANK ⌐

The Stamford Savings Bank
Stamford, CA

The Lowell Five
Lowell, MA

First Tennessee Bank National Corporation
Memphis, TN

Eastland Savings Bank
Woonsocket, RI

First National Bank & Trust Company
Washington, PA

South Holland Trust & Savings Bank
South Holland, IL

Branch Banking & Trust Company of South Carolina
Greenville, SC

Dai-ichi Kangyo Bank of California
Los Angeles, CA

Bank of West Baton Rouge
Port Allen, LA

CoreStates Financial Corporation
Philadelphia, PA

Tokai Bank of California
Irwindale, CA

Southern California Bank
Downey, CA

Chino Valley Bank
Chino, CA

Tompkins County Trust Company
Ithaca, NY

Colonial American National Bank
Roanoke, VA

Central Bank
Meriden, CT

National City Bank
Cleveland, OH

Union National Bank of Texas
Laredo, TX

Boulevard Bank
Chicago, IL

Boulevard Bank

Peoples Westchester Savings Bank
Hawthorne, NY

National Savings Bank
Albany, NY

Lexington Federal Savings Bank
Lexington, KY

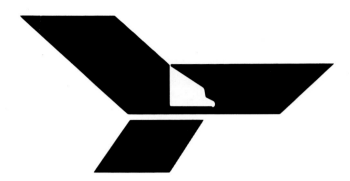

American Federal Savings & Loan
Anderson, IN

First Community Bancshares
Princeton, WV

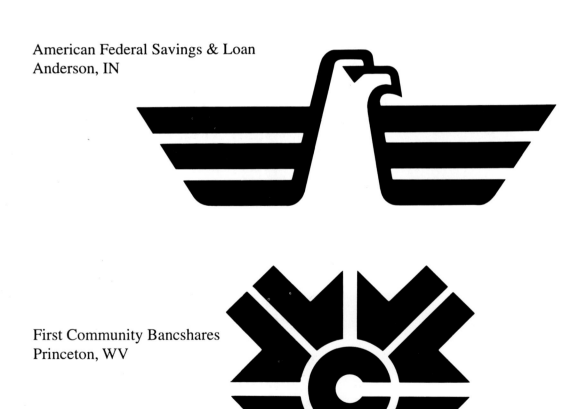